T0158975

MY CHRISTMAS OF MIRACLES

AND OTHER SHORT STORIES ABOUT ORGAN TRANSPLANT

Mary Jarrett Saubert

InspiringVoices®
A Service of **Guideposts**

Inspiring Voices books may be ordered through booksellers or by contacting:

Inspiring Voices
1663 Liberty Drive
Bloomington, IN 47403
www.inspiringvoices.com
1-(866) 697-5313

Because of the dynamic nature of the Internet, any web addresses or links contained in this book may have changed since publication and may no longer be valid. The views expressed in this work are solely those of the author and do not necessarily reflect the views of the publisher, and the publisher hereby disclaims any responsibility for them.

Any people depicted in stock imagery provided by Thinkstock are models, and such images are being used for illustrative purposes only.

Certain stock imagery © Thinkstock.

ISBN: 978-1-4624-0287-8 (sc)
ISBN: 978-1-4624-0288-5 (e)

Library of Congress Control Number: 2012914915

Printed in the United States of America

Inspiring Voices rev. date: 9/24/2012

Contents

Preface

I have been a Registered Nurse since 1972. Throughout the years, many situations have occurred that have inspired me and engrained themselves in my memory. I would like to share a few of them with you in the hopes that they may remind each one of us that every day is a gift of life to be lived to the fullest.

Most of the people I have chosen to write about are organ transplant recipients. Their stories are all true. Some are sad, some are funny, but all of them show how precious life is.

When possible, I have obtained the consents of people named in this book. In the event that I was unable to locate anyone or a relative of that person, the name has been changed to protect their identities.

Introduction

For years, my friends have been telling me I needed to write a book. Indeed, I actually had a file in my computer labeled 'Mary's Book' but never thought I would do anything with it until I received the email from Inspiring Voices announcing their book contest. I decided to select stories that had made a difference in my life with the hope that they could inspire other people as well.

As a transplant nurse, I truly believe in the gift of life, and by sharing these true stories about real, everyday people and how organ donation saved their lives, I hope to inspire others to consider signing cards to become organ donors.

I also want to give hope to people who are waiting to receive life saving transplants.

I would like to emphasize that the majority of transplant recipients do not encounter the huge number of problems that some of the patients in my stories have had to overcome but please realize that, as a nurse, the patients who I get to know the best are the patients who are in the hospital the longest.

GEORGE

GEORGE HAD BEEN WAITING for several years for a lung transplant. The rules at the time basically stated that after he was accepted as a candidate for transplant, he waited his turn to be transplanted and hoped the call came before he died.

In George's case, it did not look like he would be able to hang on much longer although he had fought valiantly. As his lung disease progressed, he had become weaker until he was no longer able to walk. Recently, it was even difficult for him to eat since the act of chewing and swallowing required more oxygen than his lungs could process.

George had been in the hospital for the last month receiving high flow oxygen, tube feedings, IV's, and physical therapy, but still, his body continued to fail. Finally, his doctor told George and his family that it was time to move to Hospice.

Within hours of his transfer, a lung became available that matched George. By now, George was in and out of consciousness but the doctor was able to explain the situation to George, cautioning that he might not be strong enough to survive the surgery.

George decided he had nothing to lose by trying. Miraculously, he sailed through the surgery and was out of ICU and back in his room within a matter of days. The day he arrived back on my unit, I had a student nurse working with me. I was pleased to see that George was a healthy pink color and was not wearing oxygen. He broke into a big smile as he said, "Look at me! I can breathe and talk at the same time!"

"How would you like to go for a walk?" I asked.

Surprise and shock filled his eyes as he said, "I'm not trying to be uncooperative, Mary, but I haven't walked for almost a year. I don't think I can. I'm happy just the way I am."

"Well, I'm not," I said. "The longer you wait, the harder it will be. You didn't get a transplant so you could stay in bed, did you?"

Hesitantly, he agreed. The student looked a bit skeptical but followed my lead. I promised we would hold him securely and that he wouldn't fall. Slowly, we helped him sit up, taking care not to hurt him and allowing his body to adjust to the change in position. When we were convinced that he was not dizzy and that all was well, we gently lowered his legs to the floor and, with one of us on either side, slowly stood him up. Sweat broke out on his forehead and he grasped us firmly, not quite believing what was happening.

With my arm around him, I gently rocked his body so that one foot lifted off the floor and landed several inches in front of him. I said, "George, you just took a step! How did that feel?" The smile on his face said it all. We then helped him back to bed.

Around midnight, George's call light came on. When I entered the room he asked, "Can we take another walk?" This time we took two steps. Each day, he was able to take a few more steps, and with much help from physical therapy, he was soon walking a few steps at a time with a walker.

Finally, he was able to stand up without help and was ready to go home. He continued to improve until he could walk totally normally. George eventually resumed a healthy life and continues to do well.

JOE

M Y HUSBAND AND I had tickets to a big race, and as luck would have it, I was scheduled to work the night before. Normally, someone would have traded with me but it seemed everyone who had the day off also had plans. The best that I could hope for was the possibility of leaving a few hours early.

Those hopes were dashed when I arrived to work the night before the race. Within 5 minutes, we received three new patients. Two of them were to receive kidney transplants within a few hours and the third patient was very confused and needed constant supervision. Many of the other patients on the floor were very ill and needed a lot of attention as well.

We all pitched in and finally got all of the crises under control and the workload on an even keel. It looked like I might be able to slip out an hour early, which was better than nothing.

I was headed toward the elevator when another nurse ran after me, saying there was a phone call for me. The lady on the phone was crying and asking for me specifically.

It was my friend Susan. Susan had received a lung transplant several years before, and through the Transplant Support Group, we had become friends.

Susan stated that her brother Joe was in the ICU and was not expected to live through the night. She asked if I would come and sit with her.

When I arrived, Joe was propped up on pillows and had an oxygen mask on but his lips, hands and feet were blue, swollen, and cold. His blood pressure was 60/30. Every breath was a struggle, followed by a long pause, and it was doubtful if he would take another one.

After I had been there about twenty minutes, he slowly opened his eyes, pulled his oxygen mask off, sat up, and looked at each person in the room as if to impress their images in his mind.

As his lips parted, total silence descended on the room as we all leaned forward so we could hear him if he spoke.

He said, "Do you think they'll show the race on TV today?"

Joe miraculously recovered fully and returned home. As far as I know, he is still doing well.

REMEMBERING PATTY

I WOKE UP ON MY day off thinking of Patty. No matter how hard I tried to focus on my errands, she still dominated my thoughts. Finally, I decided, that despite my promise to myself to separate work from my private life, I needed to go see her…if she was even still alive.

As I drove to the hospital, I reflected on how this extraordinary little woman had affected so many other lives. She was truly an example of how one person can make a difference.

I remembered when I met her. In shift report, I had learned that Patty was being admitted for evaluation for a double lung transplant. She had received a kidney transplant several years before but the disease that had caused her kidneys to fail had now attacked her lungs.

Later that day I was walking past her room when her call light came on. Although I wasn't assigned to her, I went in to see if there was something I could do for her. Luckily for me, she was facing away from me because my jaw dropped open in shock when I saw her tiny, emaciated body curled up in a fetal position. Had I not known better, I would have thought she was about nine years old. Her gown had fallen off her shoulders revealing every rib and vertebrae.

I managed to compose myself and ask if I could help her. Again, I was taken by surprise as the tiny face turned toward me with the most radiant, glowing smile I had ever seen. The room literally lit up as she asked me to help her to the bathroom.

I stammered as I asked, "Are you sure you can get up? I mean, what can I do to help you get up?"

Patiently, she explained what I needed to do. In the end, I actually picked her up and carried her although I made sure her feet were on the floor so she could think she was helping.

I got her tucked back in bed and was leaving when she playfully jabbed one tiny, contractured hand several times in my direction, chiding, "Uh, uh, uh! You can't leave without putting a pillow between my knees."

That became our little joke. Whenever she saw me, she would shake her fist and say, "Uh, uh, uh"…and we would finish the sentence together.

There was a lot of discussion and controversy in the weeks that followed as to whether precious lungs should be transplanted into a person who would never be able to walk or take care of herself. Her disease was so far advanced that, in all likelihood, other major organs would soon fail. Oblivious to all of the talk, Patty's face would light up as she made plans for her life 'after I get my lungs'.

Although she was unable to walk and never left her room except for tests, word spread about this feisty little woman with the radiant smile and uplifting personality. Soon, doctors and other hospital personnel who had no connection to her case were stopping by just to meet her. I have never seen anything like this happen before.

I was her nurse when she had a terrible drug reaction and had to be transferred to the ICU. Her ravaged body could not recover and I had heard that she had been transferred to Hospice.

So, here I was, for some reason driven to visit her.

When I arrived, her teenage son and her father were with her. Although they had rarely been able to visit her, she had proudly told us all about her son. Her father had called her on the phone nearly every day.

I introduced myself and explained that I had been one of Patty's nurses. Her Dad gave me a friendly nod. Patty was in a coma and looked very peaceful although her breathing indicated to me that death was not far off.

With tears coursing down my cheeks, I asked her Dad if he would mind if I placed a pillow between her knees. Hesitantly, he said that the nurses had just gotten her comfortable and were taking good care of her.

I agreed with him and then told him about our little joke and that I had promised her I would always make sure she had a pillow between her knees. He nodded his approval.

I tucked the pillow in place gently, said goodbye, and was surprised to see her Dad rise to walk me to the elevator. I thanked him for his kindness.

Later, I learned that a short time later, Patty had passed away… with the pillow between her knees. To this day, I am in awe as I think of how this tiny little lady who could not walk or even feed herself had impacted so many peoples' lives based totally on her positive attitude.

JAKE

I HAD ENJOYED SEVERAL DAYS off and arrived to work amidst a chorus of "Mary, Jake is in room 10 and has been asking to see you." I saw that I was assigned to be his nurse, so as soon as I listened to report, I went to his room.

He looked the same as always, with a twinkle in his eye and a grin that predicted that a joke or prank was about to be unveiled. His wife and sister were with him, as usual.

"Well, Jake, I hear you've been asking for me. What can I do for you?"

"I just wanted to know if you had any more of those electric fly swatters you had at the picnic," he said.

"Yes, as a matter of fact, I do. Would you like red, blue, or yellow?"

For the next few minutes, we talked about how much fun electric fly swatters were and how mine, with the triple screens, were far superior to those with a single screen. I told them a funny story about how I nearly got thrown out of a restaurant when I demonstrated one to some friends by executing a black olive. The manager heard the popping noise and thought I was shooting a gun. We all laughed at that.

Later, when his wife and sister went to the cafeteria, I said, "Jake, I think there is something more important than electric fly swatters you want to talk about, isn't there?"

He said, "Yes, I'm dying. There's nothing else they can do for me."

"I am very, very sorry to hear that," I said. "I will try to answer your questions. What do you need to ask me?"

"Mary, I'm not afraid to die. I knew my lung transplant wouldn't last forever, but it's done a pretty good job for me for all of these years. I made the most of my time since the transplant and I'm ready to accept that it's over, but my wife isn't. I want you to talk to her for me."

"I'll try, but I'm not exactly sure I understand what you want me to discuss with her. Do you think she's denying that you're dying? Is that the problem?"

"No, not really. She knows I'm dying. She was in the room when the doctor talked to us. I know she doesn't want me to die but at some point she will have to accept it. I have everything in order for her so I know she will be ok financially. She and my sister have always been best friends so I know she will have lots of support. My sister will be there to help her care for our (quadriplegic) son. She has had to take care of him and me at the same time since I have been sick, so I know she will be able to do it."

"There are two big problems you can help me with. I want to be an organ donor so I can help others like someone helped me and I want a big funeral with lots and lots of people."

"OK," I said, "let's talk about the organ donation first. I will talk to the Organ Procurement Organization tonight to see if the rules have changed, but as far as I know, it is not likely that any of your organs can be transplanted because the anti-rejection medicines you have been on all these years usually cause some damage. However, it is possible that your corneas, skin, and tissues might be suitable for transplant."

With that, his face lit up. "My Dad started the cornea program in our city and it would make me very happy knowing that I could help someone see again."

"I should have some answers for you tonight about that. Have you talked to your wife about your funeral?"

"I've tried. She doesn't plan to even have a funeral for me. No funeral, no viewing, nothing. You know me! I know everyone in town and have a good time wherever I am. I want my funeral to be a celebration. My friends will be disappointed."

"Now that you're in the hospital, do you think she might be more likely to talk about it with you?" I asked.

"Nope. I've been in here a few days already and have tried. She walks out of the room. That's why I asked for you. I don't know how much time I have and I want to be sure this is taken care of before I go."

"Jake, we have a chaplaincy department here that deals with issues like this. Why don't I call them for you?"

"No, no! I know you and trust you. I know you can convince her."

I was starting to feel a bit panicky at this point. Organ donation questions I could deal with but convincing his wife of something this important when he couldn't was a huge assignment. This was way out of my comfort zone. What if I failed? What could I say? Where could I even start?

I took a deep breath and said, "I am working the next three nights. Let me think about this and try to get a plan together. I'll talk to the organ procurement people tonight for sure and will try to talk to your wife, but Jake, I can't promise I can convince her."

"Okay, I know you'll do your best. Thank you."

Before the night was over, between taking care of my other patients, I did call organ procurement and got answers for him. No, he couldn't donate his organs, but he could donate corneas, skin, and some tissues.

That night, I tossed and turned and woke up no closer to having a plan than before. When I returned to work, Jake was definitely weaker and more short of breath.

Later that evening, I saw his wife looking out the window at the end of the hall. I knew this was my chance. She rarely left his side and when she did, Jake's sister was usually with her.

I tried to look nonchalant as I greeted her. Hi, Marg, how are you today?"

"Okay, I guess."

"This is hard, isn't it?"

"Yes. I don't know what I'll do without him. We've been together for so long."

"The two of you were inseparable," I added. "You could finish each other's sentences and always seemed like you were having so much fun. I wish I had known you both before Jake got sick."

"I know," she replied. "But now I don't know what to say to him."

I gathered my courage and took a deep breath. "Marg, Jake is feeling the same way. He would really like to talk to you about his funeral."

She started crying and shook her head. "I can't," she sobbed.

I touched her arm and stood there with her, then quietly said, "This is very important to him. He asked me to talk to you about it."

"I know it's important to him," she said, "but I don't think I can sit through a big funeral with all of those people there."

"It will be hard," I agreed, "but what I am more worried about is that down the road I would hate to think you might regret not having had this conversation with him." I immediately hated myself for putting a guilt trip on her but it was too late to take it back now.

"Think about it," I said. "If you need to talk to me, a chaplain, or anyone else, we will do whatever we can to help you."

She nodded and slowly walked back to the room.

Later, when I entered the room, they were hand in hand and both seemed peaceful. They asked if the organ procurement organization had a plaque or anything that they could use at the funeral to indicate that Jake was a cornea and tissue donor. I agreed to find out.

"And one more thing," Marg said. "Will you come to the funeral?"

"I will if I can. If I am scheduled to work, I probably can't, but I will try."

Jake died the next day. Marg and Jake's sister were in the room with him. I was their nurse.

I did go to the funeral. The beautiful plaque was prominently displayed inside the entrance to the church.

I sat alone in the back of the large church for the service. It was packed, just as Jake had predicted. The organist played beautiful hymns. Then, there was a slight pause before Frank Sinatra belted out the words to 'I Did It My Way.'

Heads turned in surprise. Then there was a quiet chuckle, and then another as the congregation erupted in laughter.

Jake really did do it his way.

DONNIE

DONNIE WAS BEING ADMITTED to the hospital for a biopsy of a suspicious growth in his prostate. Some of the medications he was taking to prevent him from rejecting his heart transplant made him susceptible to cancer, so his doctor was taking no chances.

He had done exceptionally well after his transplant and we all wished the best for him. However we knew that this procedure was normally done as an outpatient and the fact that his doctor was admitting him to the hospital was clearly a bad sign.

I remembered the night Donnie had come in for his transplant.

We had received a call stating he would be arriving in about an hour. He was on a potent IV medication continuously at home to keep his heart pumping as efficiently as possible, but even with the medication, his cardiac output was only seven percent.

There was no doubt that he needed a heart transplant as soon as possible.

Soon, the doors to the unit burst open and a young man ran in, nervously saying that his Dad was coming in for a transplant. By the looks of the son, he was about to have his own heart attack if he didn't calm down!

We told him he had arrived before his Dad and suggested he wait in the room for his Dad to arrive but he was so nervous, he couldn't sit still. None of the nurses had time to sit with him, so I quickly went into the room of a patient who had received a heart transplant several days before and explained the situation to him.

"Maybe if he can see how well you are doing in just a few days, that will help him relax," I said. The patient was glad to help. The son listened to the patient tell his story until his Dad arrived.

About twenty minutes later, the doors opened to admit a woman in street clothes and a bearded man with a ponytail wearing flannel pajamas with little polar bears on them.

I was amazed that Donnie had walked all the way from the parking garage but he was determined to do everything himself. Soon, his room filled to overflowing with family and a multitude of friends. I decided to move the whole crowd, patient included, to the waiting room so I could do my work and his friends could all stay.

As I worked, I realized that there was a second crisis occurring in this family. Donnie and Mona's daughter had given birth to a very tiny, premature baby girl several days before. The baby was in the neonatal critical care unit at another hospital in town. It had been a tough decision for the family to leave the baby when Donnie got his call to come in for his transplant.

Donnie sailed through surgery with flying colors and was home in a little over a week. He quickly resumed his life and barbequed on the grill in his back yard the first weekend he was home.

Now, he was possibly facing another crisis.

When I arrived at work the day after the biopsy, Donnie met me in the hall with a big smile on his face. "The biopsy on my prostrate came back and it is negative," he said.

"That's wonderful!" I said, "But incidentally, the word is prostate, not prostrate."

Puzzled, he asked, "What's the difference?"

"Prostrate means to lie down flat," I answered.

Still serious, he said, "Well, it's been doing that for a number of years but I'm still glad it's not cancer."

Donnie just celebrated the ninth birthday of his granddaughter, Paige, and the ninth anniversary of his new life.

DOLORES

🐍

DOLORES AND HER HUSBAND lived in a very rural area nearly four hours from the hospital. Although they didn't even live in the same state as the hospital, this was the closest lung transplant center.

Dolores fully understood that whenever she received the call to come in for her transplant that there would not be a minute to spare. Since there was no way of knowing when that call would come, she kept a bag packed and several spare oxygen tanks by the front door at all times.

One night, the sound of the phone woke her from a deep sleep. It was the hospital. "Come as quickly as you safely can," the voice said.

Dolores woke her husband and they quickly dressed. When they opened they door, they were shocked to see a blizzard was in progress. Already, the snow was deep and drifts were all they could see.

Her husband furiously attacked the driveway in an effort to get the car out to the county road but deep in the back of his mind he doubted that they could make it to the interstate. The road had not yet been plowed and he could see no evidence of tire tracks.

Quickly, he threw the shovel in the car, grabbed Dolores' bag and oxygen, and guided her into the car. The car slid and the tires spun but it managed to inch backwards from the driveway to the road. Then they were stuck.

Dolores took the wheel while Wayne pushed, shoveled, and rocked the car. Finally, it slid out of the rut and moved forward. He took over the driving and managed to inch forward, praying that he was still on the road.

Miraculously, they made it to the entrance ramp of the interstate but it, also, had not been plowed. As the windshield wipers attacked the blowing snow, they slid, recovered, and slid again and again until they were finally inches from the interstate. They could see that one lane in each direction had been plowed but the blowing snow was quickly obliterating the path.

Then, in the distance, they saw the tiniest white light approaching. Was it a snow plow? As it got closer, they saw it was a semi.

"Well," Wayne said, "I don't know how far he is going, but at least we have his tail lights to follow and a fresh track." Meanwhile, neither of them dared to think of the precious minutes ticking away and the futility of even thinking they could make the long trip in this weather. For now, they concentrated on staying on the road and getting as far as they could as the storm continued to rage.

Minutes seemed like hours as they continued their journey. They both had headaches from the stress and concentrating to see through the blowing snow. Then Dolores spotted a sign. Could it really be the exit to the hospital?

It was! The truck was the only vehicle on the road and it had guided them exactly where they needed to go.

Dolores received her transplant that night and enjoyed many more productive years.

RUTH

WHEN THE HOSPITAL RECEIVED the call that Ruth was coming in to have a kidney transplant in a few hours, the nursing station suddenly became very quiet. Did they really say Ruth was eighty-one years old? There had to be a mistake. Why would someone of that age receive a life saving transplant when there were thousands of people half her age and even a fourth her age on the waiting list?

The answer was very interesting. Aside from her kidney failure and some hearing loss, Ruth was very healthy and active. She was actually much healthier than her husband.

The potential donor in this situation was also elderly and had always been adamant that he wanted to be an organ donor if that was at all possible. Normally, it isn't done, but in this case the donor had also been a very vigorous, vivacious man and his kidney function tested in an acceptable range. The doctors would not place his kidney in a young recipient simply because of the age of the donor and the fact that the kidney function wasn't perfect, but it was certainly working well enough to keep Ruth off dialysis and make her life much more bearable.

Ruth was told the circumstances and fully understood that this was not a perfect kidney. She also knew that the surgery would be very tough and recovery could be difficult. It was up to her to make the decision. She decided to go for it.

So here she was, pushing her husband in a wheelchair to her room. She had a big smile on her face and repeatedly thanked God for the miracle she was about to receive. She knew that most people her age did not get this opportunity.

As I prepared her for surgery, the biggest obstacle was communicating with her. In the rush to get to the hospital, she had forgotten her hearing aids.

By talking very loudly and repeating everything several times, we both struggled through as well as we could. At one point I said to her, "Ruth, I have a lot of questions to ask you. These are standard questions that we ask every patient. Even though some of the questions may not apply to you, I still have to ask. Do you understand?"

She was very agreeable. I'm sure this wasn't the first time she had encountered many of these questions.

All was well until I asked, "Do you feel threatened by anyone from a previous relationship?"

She looked at me and said, "Honey, I've been married for sixty-two years. I don't even remember a previous relationship!" We both laughed and continued with the tasks at hand.

She sailed through the x-rays, EKG, IV, and lab draws. Finally, I said to her, "Ruth, I have to give you an enema."

She had a puzzled look on her face as she said, "Oh, what kind on animal?"

"No, not an animal, an enema," I repeated, louder this time.

"Darn," she said, "I had my heart set on a kangaroo!"

Ruth received her kidney transplant and recovered remarkably quickly. She continued to care for her husband until he passed away. She went to be with him several months later.

THE SIGNIFICANCE
OF A DIME

J ACKIE PASSED AWAY FOURTEEN minutes after midnight on December 31. His goal had been to make it until January first so his wife, Judy, could collect one more check to help ease their financial burdens.

Jackie had received a lung transplant ten years before and had lived those ten years to the max. He and Judy were inseparable and their children and grandchildren were all part of their closely-knit family.

As Jackie and Judy grew older, they both experienced health problems typical of 'old age' but nothing slowed them down much until Jackie added breathing problems to his list. His transplanted lung was wearing out and his other health problems prevented him from being considered for another transplant.

On December the 20th, Jackie was admitted to the hospital with the hopes that his lung could be 'revived' with more potent medications. Unfortunately, nothing seemed to help.

Judy stayed by his side night and day. Most of the time, he was comfortable as long as he didn't move around much. His grandchildren came to see him frequently and the smallest one would sit on his bed and play with his hospital armbands.

Jackie and Judy celebrated their forty-eighth wedding anniversary by renewing their vows in the waiting room in the hospital. It was a ceremony to remember with Jackie in his suit and Judy wearing a beautiful dress. Their pastor conducted the service. The family all attended and after the ceremony, enjoyed the fellowship of ice cream and cake together.

The following day, Jackie began having more trouble breathing. He knew he would not be leaving the hospital and expressed his desire to donate 'anything someone else could use' after he was gone to repay the precious gift that an unknown person had given him ten years before. This wish was very important to him and he discussed it with many of the doctors and nurses.

Jackie took his last breath at 12:14 a.m. on New Year's Eve. Although Judy had been expecting him to pass, nothing can prepare us for the loss of a loved one. She was inconsolable. Surrounded by her family, the hospital chaplain, and the nurses, no one was able to find words that would comfort her. We all began to worry about her health as she wept uncontrollably. As she stumbled out of Jackie's room into the hall, her family followed.

I took this opportunity to slip into the room to tidy things up. As I walked past the bed, I noticed something shiny on the floor at the foot of the bed. It was a dime. I stopped and looked at it for a few seconds, then carefully picked it up and walked into the hall where Judy sat grieving.

I put my arm around her and through my own tears said, "Judy, I need to share something with you." Her tears slowed as she struggled to listen to me tell the following story: "When my Dad passed away, my friend Ruth went with me as I drove 500 long miles to attend his funeral. When Ruth took a turn driving, I fell asleep and dreamt I was sitting on a small couch in a tiny, unfamiliar room at twilight. As I rose to leave, I glanced back. I still remember the rust, olive, and taupe colors of the plaid cloth on the couch but more than that, I remember the vividly shining dime that was there. Although it was nearly dark in the room the dime was sending off twinkles of light similar to the stars in a Disney movie. As I continued to look at the dime, I realized that the light was coming from an eternal light on the back of the dime. I felt an immense peace as I realized that Dad was telling me he was in Heaven and was okay."

"When I awoke, I looked at a dime, and sure enough, there is an eternal flame on the back. After that, I started finding dimes in the most unusual places—places I had just walked by and knew for a fact that there had been no dime there seconds before."

"Judy," I said, "you are probably wondering why I am telling you this story but when I walked by Jackie's bed a few minutes ago, there was a dime on the floor at the foot of his bed and it was glowing, too."

I opened my hand and held out the dime to her. "Judy, we both know there was no dime there earlier or someone would surely have seen it. This is your dime, not mine. I hope it brings you as much peace as my dime did for me."

As her fingers closed tightly around the dime, she was able to control her sobs and allow her family to take her home without her beloved husband.

Jackie died less than 24 hours short of his goal of New Year's Day. However, if he had lived another day, I would not have been working and Judy would never have known the significance of the dime.

I lost track of Judy. I heard that their son compiled his Dad's notes into a book of Jackie's life as Jackie had planned to do. I hope Judy is still finding dimes. I still do, always when I need them most.

SANDY

MY HUSBAND HAD BEEN deployed to Iraq. We had bought expensive tickets to a sporting event and I was not looking forward to going alone. All of my friends had their own tickets, weren't interested in the event, or wanted more than one ticket. After a Transplant Support meeting, Sandy approached me and asked if she could go with me. I was hesitant, and explained to her that it could be extremely hot that day, we would have to walk a really long distance, and that our seats were up multiple flights of steps. The last thing I wanted was for her to get sick because of me.

Sandy sometimes had pain in her hip. What would we do if she got stuck halfway up the steps? I also remembered her telling me her pre-transplant story.

She had been seeing a pulmonologist for quite some time who had told her she was not a candidate for a lung transplant. One day, she felt so bad she thought she was dying. The receptionist squeezed her in for an emergency appointment and told her she would be seen by a different pulmonologist. Sandy didn't care at that point who saw her. She knew she couldn't go on like this.

After the exam, the new doctor said, "You need a lung transplant. Why haven't you been referred to a transplant pulmonologist?" An appointment was set up immediately.

The transplant team explained the requirements she would need to meet in order to be listed as a transplant candidate. She would need to have insurance or some means of payment for the testing, surgery, expensive medications, and any other medical care she would require for the rest of her life. She would also need someone, whether it was a family member or someone else, who would make a commitment to be available on a long-term basis to help her physically and emotionally when she needed it. Whomever that person was needed to clearly understand that this could be a very intensive commitment, much more than providing casseroles and making a few phone calls for the first week after she was released from the hospital. Sandy would have to undergo psychological testing to be sure she was willing and able to comply with the stress and lifelong commitment to caring for herself and her new lungs. In addition, she would have to have a myriad of medical tests, labs, and x-rays to determine that she had no other health issues that would interfere with the transplant or the medications she would be taking and that her body could survive the surgery. Last, but not least, she would have to regularly attend pulmonary rehab to exercise her muscles and keep her body and her own lungs functioning as well as they possibly could.

Her first day of pulmonary rehab consisted of her brother and a therapist holding her upright on the treadmill. The goal was for her to walk for six minutes at half a mile an hour. She wasn't even able to complete two minutes. Later, after she had had her transplant, the therapist confided to her that she never thought Sandy would be able to meet the requirements for transplant. However, Sandy was determined and continued to return to rehab for two years until she was strong enough to be transplanted.

Now, five years after transplant, she wanted to go with me to this event. She looked great and was always on the go, I knew, but pushing her great-grandbabies around the block on a shady street was a far cry from walking half a mile in the heat and humidity, climbing eight or more flights of stairs, and sitting in the broiling sun all day. However, she persisted and said, "This is on my bucket list. I may never have another chance to do this. I'll be fine."

We decided to meet at the hospital, which was about halfway between our houses and in the general vicinity of the event. We were both familiar with the parking garage there and would have a much better chance of finding each other there than at the actual event. She would bring the sandwiches and I would bring a cooler of ice water.

As I left the house the morning of the event, the temperature was already miserably hot. The weatherman predicted a high of 100 degrees by noon. Unfortunately, he was right.

I picked Sandy up at the hospital, and drove as close as I could get to a parking lot near the event. Several blocks from the parking lot, I suggested that Sandy get out and wait for me in the shade since there was no point in both of us walking all that way. That worked fine. We took our time walking to the bleachers and began the long climb. Every few flights, we would stop and rest. We were both drenched in sweat when we finally arrived in our seats.

Despite the heat, we both enjoyed the event and our time together. We had both been careful to drink lots of water all day and waited for the bleachers to empty so we wouldn't have to fight the crowd.

When we reached the spot where she had waited for me before, we both decided that had worked well, so she stayed there with the cooler and I walked the rest of the way to get the car.

When I arrived at the corner of the block where I had left her, I was dismayed to discover that the police officer directing traffic had decided to make the street one way to simplify dispersing the traffic. She was in no mood to listen to my story and would not let me get out of the car to get Sandy. Unfortunately, we had turned our cell phones off and Sandy had not yet turned hers back on. I could see her but she was not looking in my direction. I left a voice message for her and followed the policewoman's instructions to drive in the opposite direction.

Now, I was truly worried. I knew it might be several hours before I could get back to pick Sandy up. All of the roads had been temporarily turned into one-way streets to get all of the fans out as quickly as possible. There was absolutely no way to get back there.

Sandy, of all people, did not need to stand out in the boiling sun for several more hours. The shade was gone. I had no idea of what to do. Finally, after driving several miles, I pulled over at the side of the street and parked beside a police car. The policeman was directing traffic and had no time to talk to me but at least he didn't make me move.

About that time, Sandy received the message I had left on her cell phone and called me back. I explained my predicament.

She said, "Well, why don't I go ask a policeman to help me?"

I quickly advised her not to do that. "The policemen have their hands full and are even hotter than we are, standing on the black asphalt, dressed in black uniforms. My advice is to stay out of their way. They are not in good moods," I said. We hung up, promising to keep in touch until one of us had a better idea.

About five minutes later, Sandy called back. "Exactly where are you?" she asked. I gave her the street address.

"Stay right there," she said. "This nice policeman will bring me to you."

I was dumbfounded. How did she pull that one off?

A few minutes later, I saw flashing lights approaching. As the police car parked beside mine, Sandy got out and got into my car.

The officer directing traffic where I was motioned me into the traffic and asked me which direction I wanted to go. I couldn't believe my good luck.

"How did you manage to convince the policeman to drive through all that traffic and find me?" I asked.

"Well," she said, "I told him I was a lung transplant recipient and that my nurse had brought me to the event. I explained that you were directed away from our meeting spot and couldn't pick me up. I told him I couldn't stay in this heat and I needed you to take me to the hospital, so he told me to get in. So here I am."

I shook my head, not believing she had actually had the nerve to do that.

"Everything I said was absolutely true," she said. "I just didn't tell him that the only reason I needed to get to the hospital was because my car was parked there."

We still laugh about that day. Sandy is still going strong, enjoying life and doing things she never even thought about doing before her transplant.

ADRIEN

Thⁱˢ ⁱˢ ᵃ ᶜᵒᵖʸ of a prayer request I sent to all of my friends when Adrien had his heart transplant.

"I try not to bother the good Lord with problems I think I can solve myself, but occasionally something comes along that needs more than I can give.

As you know, I work with organ transplant recipients and while all of them are very ill, for most of them, the combination of motivation, hard work, and good medical and nursing care pull them back into the world but sometimes someone comes along who needs more than we can provide. We have a patient like that now on our unit and I am asking you to join me in praying for him.

Before I go any further, let me say I did discuss this with Adrien and got his full permission to share as much about him as I see fit so that you can get to know him and learn about his current situation.

Adrien is currently 23 years old. He has had heart problems since childhood. He has endured many hospitalizations and surgeries but still managed to excel academically and socially. Recently, he and his cat Phoebe moved into their first apartment and Adrien started college.

Adrien had known for years that he would need a heart transplant at some point in time. The goal, of course, was to keep his own heart functional as long as possible and delay transplant until it was absolutely necessary. Meanwhile, he completed the battery of physical and psychological tests that qualified him to be a transplant recipient. He was placed on a waiting list for a donor heart that would match his body size, blood type, and antibody level so he would not reject it. His own heart declined very rapidly during the wait and he was very near the end of his life when the call finally came that a match was available. By then, he was on some very powerful intravenous medications at home just to keep his heart beating.

When he came in for the transplant, his lungs and liver were both congested with blood because his heart could no longer pump enough blood out to his body to make room for the venous blood to return to his heart. Those factors, along with the fact that he had so much scar tissue from multiple childhood surgeries made him an extremely high risk. When those surgeries were done, no one really expected him to live to see adulthood and few heart transplants had been done on anyone in his situation. The goal at that point had simply been to keep him alive as long as possible. A heart transplant wasn't even considered to be an option for him. Consequently, his original veins and arteries had been cut off so short that it would be nearly impossible to attach the new heart. This transplant center was one of the few that would even take a chance on a person in his situation. Because he was so young and had adhered strictly to all of the many rules, the decision was made to go ahead and attempt the transplant. The doctors were hopeful that his lungs and liver would recover if and when he had a strong, healthy heart.

His transplant went well and his new heart functioned perfectly. Within weeks, the pressure in his lungs decreased. His liver, however, did not recover. Years of congestive heart failure had caused cirrhosis of the liver. So, once a week he has to have ten liters of fluid removed from his belly via a very large needle. His belly gets so tight that he looks like he might explode and the extra weight hurts his back. Liquid seeps out of his skin continuously and his belly has actually 'sprung a leak' and has fluid running out of it in a constant stream. His skin is actually peeling off his hands and feet and he has stretch marks on his belly.

Then, due to all the toxins in his body that his liver can't remove, his kidneys failed. So now, he is on dialysis three times a week. His doctors told him this week that his only hope is to have a simultaneous liver AND kidney transplant.

After the doctors left, I said to him, "Adrien, you are quite a trooper. You are the most positive person I have ever met. Many people would have given up by now but you always have a smile on your face and do everything you are asked to do. I know I couldn't be that strong."

Do you know what he said? "I have considered giving up several times but I worry about my Dad. He has been through so much and has given up so much for me that I know if I give up now it will be really hard for him."

He is on this really horrible diet to try to reduce the fluid accumulation. He can't have protein or fat because his liver can't break it down. He can't have much fluid or salt because his kidneys can't eliminate them. He is allowed to have only one meal a day and has to drink four glasses of this really nasty smelling stuff, which he does faithfully without complaining.

So, now, we are waiting for a donor who matches him who has a healthy liver and kidney. Meanwhile, every day is a challenge as his body becomes weaker and thinner. He has already had some severe internal bleeding due to his liver failure; it was a miracle that the doctors were able to stop it.

In all my years of nursing, I don't think I have met anyone with such a positive attitude and the will to live as Adrien. My heart breaks for him and I worry about him even when I am at home.

So, I ask you to pray with me that the good Lord will find a donor for him, but if it is not to be, to take him quietly and quickly with as little suffering as possible."

Please feel free to share his story with whomever you wish and to add him to all of your prayer lists."

My friends did just that. I know many prayers were said for Adrien as the prayer chain spread. For several weeks, not much changed. Then one day, I noticed that the leak in his belly had totally stopped. Gradually, he became slightly stronger. All he wanted at this point was to go home.

His doctor decided to grant this wish although I wasn't sure if he would recover or if he was going home to die.

His Dad kept us updated as he very slowly regained strength over the next year or so. Then, his kidneys slowly kicked in and started working. He tried going back to school but it was still too much for him. Although we nurses all longed to see him, he refused to come near the unit when he visited the doctor; there were too many bad memories there.

Several years later, I was at the transplant picnic and felt a tap on my shoulder. At first I couldn't place the robust, healthy young man standing in front of me. Then I realized it was Adrien. He and I spent about an hour catching up on his life. His liver was still a problem but had regained some function. The doctors still wanted him to have a liver transplant but he wanted nothing to do with it.

The following year at the picnic, he proudly told me he no longer needed a liver transplant. He was back in school full time and expects to graduate in a year. Then, he hopes to go to grad school. He works in the evenings like most college students, to help pay his tuition. Oh, and Phoebe and he still share an apartment.

Despite the fact that he had the best doctors and that they worked around the clock with Adrien's myriad of medical issues, the odds were always against his recovery.

The fact that Adrien is alive and well today is truly a testimony of the power of prayer.

BERNICE

𝄞

BERNICE'S DOUBLE LUNG TRANSPLANT had gone well. However, she had several setbacks that kept her in the hospital longer than she had planned. That didn't sit well with her at all.

Despite encouragement from her doctors and nurses that these problems were temporary, Bernice chose to handle the situation with anger. No one and no thing was exempt. The sky was too blue, there was nothing good on TV, the food was cold, her visitors stayed too long. She was livid when the nursing assistant moved her book from her bed to the table in order to put clean sheets on the bed.

The nurses tried to gently reinforce that things were not as bad as they seemed but Bernice wasn't listening. After my second twelve hour shift as her nurse, I was mentally exhausted. I sat down beside her bed and said, "Bernice, I know you are disappointed and I totally understand that. However, I personally think we each have the power to help ourselves heal by looking for the positive things that are happening around us."

"There's nothing positive happening to me," she snapped.

Ignoring that remark, I said, "Your lung transplant was a success. You no longer have to wear oxygen. You have wonderful friends who faithfully visit you. It is very obvious that they deeply care about you. Many of our patients never get visitors. Your teenage granddaughter comes every day after school to sit with you. She would rather be here with you than with her friends."

"It will take a week or so to remedy your health problems and there's nothing you or anyone else can do to speed that up but wouldn't it be much nicer to pass the time by thinking happy thoughts instead of focusing on the negative?"

"Well," she growled, "I can't think of anything positive."

I said, "Tomorrow, I will be here again for twelve hours. Every time I come in your room, I will be your trigger. Whenever you see me, I want you to think 'The world is a beautiful place'."

Grouchily, she agreed to try it. However, the very next time I entered her room, I was greeted with yet another negative comment.

"Whoa," I said. "We have an agreement. What are you supposed to think when you see me?"

Bernice furrowed her brow and thought. She raised her eyes to meet mine and slowly said, "Every time I look at you, I think, what is the world coming to?"

I couldn't help but laugh. I obviously had more work to do.

A week or so later, Bernice was well enough to go home. Two weeks after that, she was re-admitted. She had lost weight and looked awful.

I was shocked. "What happened?"

"I live by myself and didn't have the energy to do anything but get to the bathroom and take my pills."

"But what about all of your friends?" I asked. "They promised to take turns looking in on you to be sure you were OK as long as you needed them. Didn't they come?"

"Yes, at least two or three people came every day. They brought homemade casseroles and put them in the fridge."

"That was nice," I said, "but I don't understand why you lost so much weight."

"Well," she said, "I didn't have the energy to walk to the kitchen and cook them."

"It's hard for me to believe your friends wouldn't heat them for you and share a meal while they visited," I said. "I can't believe they wouldn't do that for you."

"I didn't ask them. They didn't volunteer so I figured they didn't want to."

"Bernice," I scolded, "if they went to the trouble to cook homemade meals for you and took the time to come and visit, I'm sure they would have been happy to heat them up for you, do the dishes, do the laundry, empty the trash, help you bathe, and anything else you needed help with."

For once, she had no answer.

More gently, I added, "You are usually a very self sufficient woman. Your determination is what got you through many rough spots in your life. I bet you have helped other people many times and never thought twice about it. It's hard to be on the receiving end, isn't it? "

"Most people are reluctant to come into someone else's house and rummage through cabinets, do chores, etc. without permission," I continued. "It's a little polite dance our society has created, I guess. They came to help you, but you were too proud to ask for their help. Before you go home the next time, let's have a talk with your friends."

Bernice recovered quickly, and when she went home the second time, she did allow her friends to help her. I have seen her several times in the past few years and she is thriving.

MELODY

𝄞

I GOT UP EARLY ON the morning of the Heart/Lung Transplant
Support Group picnic. When I walked outside, I was stifled by heat
and humidity. By the time I had packed everything in my car, I was so
hot and sweaty that I had to take another shower and change clothes.
I had a feeling that this was not going to be a good day. The group had
decided to have the picnic in June rather than August specifically so the
weather would be cooler but the weather today was worse than anyone
could have predicted.

Every person who had ever received a heart or lung transplant at
this hospital as well as people waiting for transplants were invited to
attend the picnic with their families. Many people were coming from
neighboring states and were probably already en route. There was no
way to cancel it now.

When I arrived at the park, I was happy to find the temperature
slightly more bearable among the beautiful shade trees but it was still
too hot and humid for anyone waiting for a transplant. Breathing for
them could be very difficult at best and this weather would make it
even harder. Furthermore, the park was nowhere near the hospital and
if anyone did get sick from the heat, we could have some big problems
on our hands.

I unpacked my vehicle and set up tables, unloaded boxes, and got
things ready. I had no sooner finished when I noticed a lady carrying
an oxygen tank laboriously walking up the slight incline toward me.
The first fact that registered in my brain was that she was a ghastly gray

color except for her mouth, ears, and hands which were dark purple. The second fact was that the top of her oxygen tank had a thick layer of ice on it from the humidity.

I quickly grabbed a chair and guided her onto it. I took her husband aside as he put his load of extra oxygen tanks down beside her and asked him if we should call an ambulance for his wife. He looked perplexed and asked why I thought she needed an ambulance.

I expressed my concern about her color and he assured me that this was her normal color. Indeed, she seemed to be breathing normally and actually had a smile on her face as she introduced herself to me and said the lady at the registration table had suggested to her that I might need help.

I wryly thought to myself that it was more likely that the lady at the registration table, herself a lung transplant recipient, had sent her in my direction because I was a nurse.

Anyway, she was here and clearly intended to stay, so I got busy finding tasks for her to do that could be done while sitting down.

Her name was Melody and her husband's name was Gregg. She was on the list for a double lung transplant and when they got the invitation to the picnic, they decided to come and investigate.

The day passed uneventfully. Miraculously, no one had any problems. Personally, I had a pounding headache by the time I got home from the heat and I suspect I wasn't alone.

Melody and Gregg became loyal members of the Support Group. Melody had been misdiagnosed by her family doctor who was insistent that her only problem was that she was overweight. At each visit, he would say, "Lose some weight and you'll be able to breathe just fine."

She made an appointment with a pulmonologist who actually told her, "You smoked when you were younger. You probably have emphysema. We can't cure that. You need to go home and get your affairs in order. You are going to die from this." Shaken but by no means ready to give up, Melody heard of a transplant pulmonologist less than an hour away. After a battery of tests, it was determined that she had pulmonary fibrosis, a disease that was quickly turning her lungs into scar tissue which prevented her lungs from transferring oxygen to her blood stream.

Melody also had pulmonary hypertension, which means the blood vessels inside the lungs had narrowed causing her heart to beat with more force in order to get blood to the lungs to pick up oxygen. This extra pressure caused hypertension inside the lungs themselves and could also cause her heart to enlarge over time.

However, before she could be transplanted, she did need to lose weight so the new lungs she would receive would not have to work so hard. She was very worried about how she would be able to lose weight when it was nearly impossible for her to exercise.

I could empathize with her. We were the same age and about the same weight. My lungs are fine and I have trouble losing weight, too. I agreed that it was going to be very difficult but it was her only hope.

First, I suggested she attend pulmonary rehab which is an exercise program tailored specifically to people with heart and lung problems. Although there were several in the state, she would have to travel quite a distance to get to any of them. However, she agreed to give it a try. She also met with a nutritionist, and Gregg agreed to support her 100%. The people in the support group did exactly what they were supposed to do and provided support in every way they could think of.

Slowly, the weight came off. It was not a moment too soon. Unfortunately, she had a very high antibody level and only 3% of the population could donate lungs to her without her body immediately rejecting them. More specifically, that is, only 3% of people with her blood type and body size who had signed their organ donor cards and lived in state could donate lungs to her that wouldn't reject. Due to her high antibody level, the donor's blood would have to undergo more tests than were normally done. Only a few labs could perform those tests in a timely manner and we had one of them at our hospital. That was why the donor needed to be in our state.

However, I could think of several patients that had been extremely difficult to match who had been successfully transplanted and were doing extremely well. The rules had changed a few years ago enabling sicker patients to move up higher on the list. Most people seemed to get transplanted in about a year and a half. Since the rules had changed, some were transplanted within months of being listed.

Melody continued to be optimistic and pushed herself to her physical limits every day to keep her body as strong as possible. At first she was encouraged as other people in the support group and in her rehab group received transplants but as time wore on, I could tell it was hard to understand why she was the only one still waiting.

Her doctor told her there had been matches but for one reason or another, none of the lungs had been suitable for transplant. They were too small, too big, damaged, diseased, ruined from cigarette smoke, etc. He reassured her that there was a match out there for her somewhere. She had been called to come in once only to be sent home when those lungs, too, were found to be unsuitable.

Meanwhile, several years passed. Her condition worsened despite her efforts. She was admitted to an intensive care unit and placed at the top of the list. There was only one more trick to pull out of the bag and it was a long shot. There was a new medicine out there that was not yet approved for pre-lung transplant patients. All sorts of hoops would have to be jumped through and mountains of paperwork would have to be approved, and quickly. At the very last second, approval was obtained and she started receiving the medicine intravenously. Slowly, over a period of weeks, her breathing eased as the dose was increased to the maximum. Gregg had to receive training to change the IV dressings and replace the bags of medicine, keeping everything sterile. Despite the reprieve, I knew that her lungs would continue to deteriorate and now there was no Plan B.

By now, she had been waiting for over six years for a transplant. Unbelievable. The whole situation was unbelievable. The fact that no match had been found, the fact that she was still alive, and the fact that she was still on her feet and optimistic after all these years was unbelievable. As time passed, her lips turned black, her ears and hands darker purple, and her legs were purple and numb from the knees to her toes. Still, she insisted on climbing the stairs to the bedroom, helped with cooking, went to rehab and to church.

Meanwhile, I was planning to retire. "Promise me you won't retire until I get my lungs," she begged. For once, I was speechless. Another member of the group spoke up and said, "I'm sure Mary will be right there with you whether she is working or not."

Actually, I wanted nothing more than to know she was transplanted before I retired. That would be a very happy way to end my career. Meanwhile, it was getting harder and harder to think of what to say to Melody when I saw her. After six years of saying, "Hang in there, stay positive, etc.," the words were beginning to sound hollow. Melody had been hanging in there and was being positive but it didn't seem to be making much of a difference. Nurses are used to fixing things and making people feel better. I couldn't think of anything more to do to help Melody and I was getting very, very worried about how this was going to turn out.

Five weeks before my last day, I arrived at work and looked at my assignment. In addition to my other patients, I would be sending someone for a lung transplant. The patient hadn't arrived yet. I asked the charge nurse if she knew the patient's name. "It's a woman, and I think it's Melanie or something like that. It's not confirmed yet."

"Please, I prayed, let it be Melody." It was. Of all times, Gregg was working that day in another part of the state so her son was more than happy to bring her to the hospital. Gregg, their pastor, and multitudes of their adult children, grandchildren, and friends, soon joined them.

Time seemed to drag by for me despite all of the work that had to be completed to get Melody ready for surgery. I knew that there were many extra tests that needed to be done and the results would have to be just right. The lungs would have to be maintained longer than normal until the surgeon gave the green light.

The other variable in Melody's case was that she was so incredibly ill. Of course, everyone who needs a double lung transplant is very ill, but few survived to this point. I knew there was a possibility that her body might not be able to accept the stress of major surgery.

Finally, all the tests were completed and the surgery was a go. I gave her a big hug as she left for the operating room. I finished my shift and then went to sit with Gregg until we knew the surgery had been completed and was a success.

Things were still touch and go for several weeks. Her kidneys failed, then recovered. She was given sedation to keep her quiet so the machines could do the work while her body slowly repaired itself. No one knew for sure that she would be able to breathe on her own or if she would be normal mentally.

Finally, the sedation was withdrawn. She moved everything which was a relief but, since she still had the breathing tube in her throat, she couldn't talk. I handed her pen and paper, but we couldn't figure out what she was trying to tell us. Gregg and I took turns guessing everything we could think of, to no avail. Finally, I said to her, "Melody, you're writing from right to left. Are you writing Chinese?"

The meaning of the look she shot me was unmistakable! Gregg and I laughed tears of joy. The old Melody was still with us.

Melody recovered fully in record time. She was released from the hospital the day before my retirement party but insisted on attending. She walked without oxygen all the way from the parking garage and stayed for the entire party.

Nowadays, it's hard to find her. She and Gregg have traveled all over the United States visiting friends and relatives. They take their grandchildren camping.

On their refrigerator is a crayon drawing of Melody from her youngest granddaughter. The face is drawn with a pink crayon and the lips are bright red.

My Christmas
of Miracles

W HO SAYS MIRACLES NO longer occur? Last Christmas, I experienced five miracles in two days. They occurred in different magnitudes and intensities, but they were miracles all the same.

Although I had retired in April, I still fill in for staffing emergencies and to help my nurse friends when they need time off. Due to the holidays, I had been working full time for several weeks. On December 23rd, I had done a lot of errands before going to work and had been all over town as I rushed to the grocery, the bank, the recycling dumpster, and performed some housework. Several hours into my shift, I realized I was missing an earring. It was my favorite Christmas earring, of course. I kept my eyes open for the rest of the shift but didn't find it; nor was it in my car, the garage, or the house when I got home.

The next day was Christmas Eve and I was called back to work. As I walked through the parking garage, there was my earring, right in the traffic path. No one had driven over it or thrown it away. While this may not be a miracle in the grand scheme of things, to me it was Miracle #1.

Several hours later, still on Christmas Eve, we got word that there might be a double lung transplant occurring in a few hours. The potential recipient was a fairly young man named Chuck who had been on a ventilator for several days. The doctor had told his wife, Chrissy, that if lungs weren't available by the next day, that he would not survive.

His doctor happened to be on our floor and I asked him if the patient's wife was here. She was. I asked another nurse to watch my patients while I went to see if Chrissy had someone with her to give her the support she needed. Luckily, she did have several people with her but was glad to meet me and welcomed any words of wisdom I could offer to help her get through the long night of worry and waiting that was ahead of her. As you can imagine, her emotions were all over the place. One minute, she was trying to cope with the probability that her husband might be dying, and now, suddenly, there was hope that he would receive a transplant. That was Miracle #2.

I returned to my floor and was talking to De, another patient, and her sister about what Chrissy was going through and suggested to De's sister that she could be of some comfort if she was willing to meet Chrissy and sit with her a while. Immediately, De said, "I want to go, too!"

I was a bit hesitant. De was making giant strides since her own lung transplant but, she, too, had been very ill at the time of her surgery and had overcome monumental obstacles to get to her current state. Although she had made a lot of progress, she was still so weak that it took two people to help her stand up and she had not yet been out of her room except to go to tests.

I asked her doctor, (the same one) what he thought about De visiting Chrissy and he enthusiastically gave his OK. "I think that would be good for her," he said.

De was so excited! She put on makeup for the first time in a long time and insisted on hair spray. Finding hair spray presented a challenge until Kathy, the unit secretary, produced some out of her locker.

When she was finally ready, we got her in a wheelchair, put a mask on her, and she and her sister took off. When they didn't come back for two hours, I was getting a bit worried, but when they returned, De was absolutely glowing. She had not only been able to provide comfort and hope to Chrissy but had also been able to realize how valuable she had been to Chuck's family when they heard her story and could see how great she looked. This visit gave De the drive and ambition she needed to complete her own convalescence. That was Miracle #3.

Meanwhile, another one of my patients was very disappointed that he had to stay in the hospital over Christmas. The doctors had sent everyone home that could safely be released but there were still about 15 people that were too ill to leave the hospital. Larrick had been in the hospital for several weeks already and had been in and out of the ICU multiple times. He was definitely doing much better now but still needed to stay a few more days with us. One of his sons who was about 12 years old, had been staying overnight with Larrick which was good for both of them. That afternoon, several of Larrick's older children had come in and erected and decorated a big, artificial tree in his room. Later, more family arrived with several large bags full of gaily wrapped packages that they put in the closets and shower. I assumed they were planning a family Christmas the next afternoon.

I was in Larrick's room just before midnight when the door opened. In walked his wife followed by their seven year old son, rubbing his eyes and stumbling with tiredness. While the rest of the family had been able to visit, he had not, due to his age. When he saw his Dad, the looks of sheer joy and love on both of their faces was indescribable. He flew across the room and with his coat and mittens still on, thrust the card he had made for his Dad into his hand. The Dad eagerly tore open the envelope and proclaimed this the best Christmas card he had ever seen and instructed his son to put it on the tree. The little boy ran to the tree, and on his tippy toes, placed the card as close to the top as he could reach, all the while grinning as only a seven year old with missing front teeth can do.

He then snuggled up in bed next to his Dad while Mom produced sandwiches, cookies, and hot chocolate from a hamper. They proceeded to have a wonderful little midnight party.

After everyone was asleep, Santa quietly got the gifts from their hiding places and put them under the tree. During the night, as other hospital personnel entered the room to do their work, I met them at the door and made them promise to do their work quietly and in near darkness so the little boy would not be awakened. Unfortunately, I was not there in the morning to see the look on the little boy's face when he realized that Santa had found him in the hospital, but I can only imagine.

I thank God that I was able to witness this because it truly was Miracle #4.

On Christmas afternoon, someone from work called me at home to report that Chuck had received his lungs and was doing great and that yet another man, Wayne, was coming in to receive lungs which was Miracle #5.

So, when people say to me how sad it is that I have to work on Christmas, I will tell them about my Christmas of 2011, my Christmas of Miracles.

Chuck, De, and Wayne have all resumed their normal lives and look and feel great. Larrick, sadly, was not able to recover and passed away. I am so glad he was able to enjoy Christmas with his family.

Afterword

There are currently thousands of people actively listed for organ transplants in the United States. Only a fraction of them will receive transplants due to a shortage of donor organs.

My hope is that 'MY CHRISTMAS OF MIRACLES AND OTHER SHORT STORIES ABOUT ORGAN TRANSPLANT' has helped dispel some myths, answered some questions, and inspired you to consider organ donation.

Organ donation is not an option everyone chooses and I respect that. Whatever your choice, please make it known to your family so that they will know your wishes and be able to abide by them if the need arises. Giving the gift of life to others can make the loss of a loved one more bearable by knowing that something good came out of a tragedy.

Printed in the United States
By Bookmasters